D1366305

SPILLVILLE

Text by Patricia Hampl

Engravings by Steven Sorman

MILKWEED EDITIONS
MINNEAPOLIS
1987

Northfield Public Library
Northfield, MN 55057

57-3550

Publication of this book is made possible by grant support from the Literature Program of the National Endowment for the Arts, the Northwest Area Foundation, and the Dayton Hudson Foundation, and by sponsorship from the Minnesota Center for Book Arts.

90 89 88 87   4 3 2 1

SPILLVILLE

© TEXT BY PATRICIA HAMPL

© ENGRAVINGS BY STEVEN SORMAN

ALL RIGHTS RESERVED. PUBLISHED 1987.

PRINTED IN THE UNITED STATES OF AMERICA

PUBLISHED BY MILKWEED EDITIONS

POST OFFICE BOX 3226

MINNEAPOLIS, MINNESOTA 55403

LIBRARY OF CONGRESS CATALOG CARD NUMBER: 86–60749

ISBN: 0–915943–16–6 LIMITED EDITION

ISBN: 0–915943–17–4 PAPER

ISBN: 0–915943–18–2 CLOTH

In Memory
of
Brenda Ueland

In Memory
of
Robert Kutak

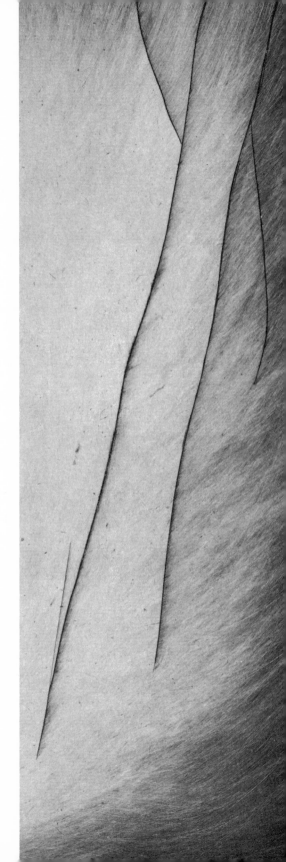

THEN

On Monday, June 5, 1893, Antonín Dvořák stepped off the noon branch line train coming from the Iowa river town of MacGregor, onto the station platform of the village of Calmar in the northeastern part of the state. He was accompanied by his wife Anna and her widowed sister Mme. Terezie Koutecká, along with the six Dvořák children, a housemaid, and Dvořák's secretary Josef Kovařík.

They had travelled from New York directly to Chicago in an impressive thirty-six hours which suited Dvořák's passion for locomotives and confirmed his respect for American casualness about its vast geography: "The state of Iowa to which we are going is thirteen hundred miles from New York, but here such distance is nothing."

In Chicago, they changed to the Chicago-St. Paul line (via Dubuque), covering the 250 miles to MacGregor in eleven hours, as if to prove that all movement naturally became more tedious and harder won in the heartland. The long ride to Mac-Gregor gave Dvořák his first view of the Mississippi, which he was eager to see. The last leg, on the slow branch line, took him away from the river, into the farmland and forest of northeastern Iowa, through an area sometimes called Little Switzerland, a wedge of Wisconsin/Iowa/Minnesota missed by the great prehistoric glacier that flattened the surrounding landscape.

In Calmar the travellers were met by Father Thomas Bílý, like most of his flock, a Czech immigrant, and by Jan Kovařík who, besides being Josef's father, was Father Bílý's choirmaster and organist at St. Wenceslas Church in Spillville, a hamlet still smaller than Calmar, which lacked railroad service. The group made the five-mile trip back to Spillville in two buggies borrowed for the occasion.

Dvořák was spending two years as director of the National Conservatory of Music in New York and had been persuaded by his secretary to spend the long summer vacation in his home-town in Iowa. Spillville, the younger Kovařík said, would provide the Master (as he faithfully called Dvořák) with the peace and quiet he needed for composition. Besides, it was a Czech settlement where he would hear his own language spoken on the street. He would be at home.

Kovařík knew his man. "Spillville will remain a happy memory for the rest of our lives," Dvořák wrote some weeks before they left the town.

They stayed the whole summer, an unusually hot one, past Dvořák's fifty-second birthday, which fell on the feast of the Nativity of Mary, September 8. He passed out cigars to the townspeople who gathered for a celebration in his honor. Two days later—quite suddenly it seemed to some people—he and his family packed up and were gone, back the long way they had come.

NOW

Driving through Iowa, mid-May. On both sides of the highway, pale green lines of sprouted soybeans run through the black furrows like basting threads. It doesn't take long to get where we're headed. We could have made it a day trip, a few hours down, a look around, back home to St. Paul before midnight. But we're stringing it out for a couple of days, the four of us friends, having knocked off work (the three adults) and school (the little girl).

"I'm sorry I'm not here," my voice is saying on the answering machine at home. "I've been called out of town on business." Even the weather seems in favor of absenteeism. A final skim of winter ice hangs somewhere high in the air, harmlessly. The day glistens.

I don't know exactly where we are, what road this is. Don't have to: I'm not driving. I'm just staring out the window. We keep dipping off the freeway to smaller, less direct routes, as if we didn't want to arrive anywhere in particular. The aimlessness of perfect travel.

But there is a destination. The rhyme of the name—Spillville—makes it sound imaginary, a town dedicated to accidents or, perhaps, populated by unusually effusive people, gushers, jabberers, tell-all types. A place of waterfalls and revelations. Not likely.

On the road-map its black dot is cast in the minute type size reserved for out-of-the-way places, twelve miles down the road from Decorah's bigger blue circle. One of the nowhere places, reticent not from the need for secrecy, but from an ingrained anonymity. But that's where we're going. Where Dvořák went just about this time of year.

I suppose that makes this trip a pilgrimage: in the footsteps of. . . .

THEN

NOW

I
LANDSCAPE

II
STUDIO

III
THE FALLS

I
LANDSCAPE

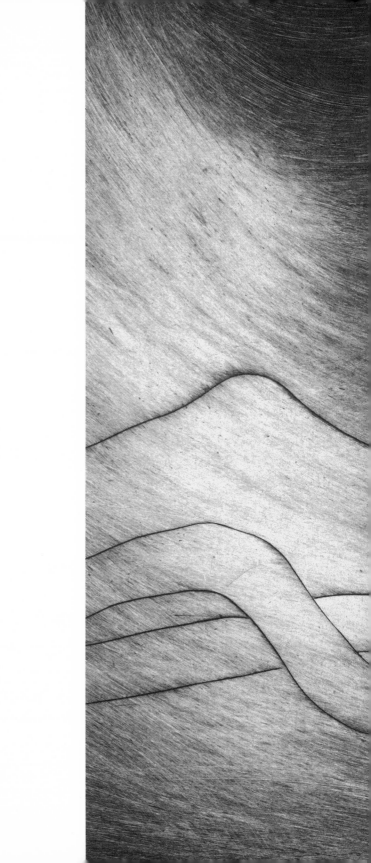

PILGRIMAGE

God, the sky is blue, and the air is shot with gold. A moment ago, we passed a farmyard where a girl about twelve, wearing a blue-and-white dress, stood waving, dwarfed by a lilac bush whose blossoms were already rusted. She seemed to beckon, but of course she was just waving at the world—us—passing by. She would have been alarmed if we'd stopped. But the impression remains that she was inviting us in.

Now, down another side road, we've decided to stop for a picnic, spreading our provisions on a patch of rocky pasture overlooking the clean geometry of the fields below. Pilsner Urquell in green bottles, the heavy-gold of Bohemian hops; cheese and salami set out on butcher paper, sweating in the sun. We rip off hunks of sourdough from a big loaf, grimacing like men tearing the Manhattan telephone directory in half. For dessert, there's Belgian chocolate so bitter it makes my eyes hurt.

This trip is a variation on a theme. Even for Dvořák, the theme was already stated; even he was making a pilgrimage. He sought the familiarity of his own language in the wilderness of English, and he came to the farmland and woods Kovařík promised would remind him of Bohemia. A good place to compose, away from the city. All that, true enough.

But he sought as well, I think, the higher pitch, the experience of immigration itself. He could have found peace and quiet closer to New York. He could even have found other Czechs nearer to hand. But he could not have replicated his countrymen's experience of immigration without crossing the wider stretch of land.

Dvořák understood (it is clear from his letters) that poverty, not idealism, was the heart of immigration. "The poorest of the poor," he said, describing the background of the settlers of Spillville. He spent most of his afternoons in Spillville, after his work was done for the day, talking to the oldest townspeople. He wanted to hear their stories.

Dvořák came not to *be* an immigrant—that was of course not possible for such a celebrated man—but he could touch the experience, at least the hem of its cloak. Perhaps his coming here is best understood as an oblique homage paid to immigration, the cruel/kind song that beguiled so many of his people. The summer of 1893 he made his brief bow to what he knew was not only his countrymen's emigration, but their banishment.

The paradox: there can be no pilgrimage without a destination, but the destination is also not the real point of the endeavor. Not the destination, but the willingness to wander in pursuit characterizes pilgrimage. Willingness: to hear the tales along the way, to make the casual choices of travel, to acquiesce even to boredom. That's pilgrimage—a mind full of journey.

It's an *adagio* movement, the slow lyrical mode of travel. Everything fits. As now, lying here, eyes closed, winter face to the spring sun. Flies, attracted to the sticky smell of flat beer left in the green bottles, are making a low sizzling sound near my head. A wasp has zoned in on the salami, and I realize, touching my hand to my forehead, that my brow is furrowed.

Somebody has put Dvořák's *American* quartet on the tape-deck, and turned the volume up to the max. Our theme song, the piece he sketched his first few days in Spillville. The *scherzo*, modelled on the song of the scarlet tanager, is drilling itself over the pasture. A happy man wrote that.

Dvořák ventured this far from home; the American Midwest was the furthest reach of his travels. Such an unlikely explorer. He was so hopelessly daunted by the carriage traffic in Prague, it is said, that he would ask a student to help him cross the street. What kind of pilgrim is that?

A fearful one, the most authentic kind.

VYSOKÁ

Dvořák wanted to understand what he was getting into. In New York he told Josef Kovařík to draw him a map of the town, with every street, every house, the name of every person and what each did for a living. The prudent pilgrim, looking before he leapt.

Then, map in hand, he was all decision. When other friends tried to convince him to spend the summer in South Carolina, he said no, he was going to Kovařík's hometown, to Spillville in Iowa. "Our summer Vysoká," he called it, linking it with the name of the country place he bought in 1884 near the Bohemian mining town of Příbram where, on clear days, he could see the foothills of the Bohemian Forest in the distance.

He drank beer with the coal miners there in the local tavern a few blocks from the old granary he had converted into a house. Dvořák was the son of a village butcher. He liked his game of *darda* in the evening and didn't care for smart city life.

Prague, London, and New York were for the business of music, for performing, teaching, all of that. But music itself belonged to Vysoká, to the forest and—especially—to the birds.

No, beyond the birds. Music belonged to sound, the endless voiced revelation of God's nature. Birds, wind, moving water. At Vysoká he kept pigeons, going first to them when he arrived in the country, to hear their low cooing. Their habits interested him, he said. And when a polecat once got into the pigeon coop and killed them all, Dvořák had the birds buried in the front yard at Vysoká because, he said, they were his friends.

Kovařík assured him: there would be pigeons in Spillville. In fact, there were no pigeons, but there were other birds. Nor were there locomotives or ocean steamers, the two great *basso* sounds he pursued in Prague and New York. All the previous year, he walked from his rented house on Seventeenth Street to Central Park to listen to the birds.

But there was too much noise. He couldn't hear the individual sounds—not birds, not wind, not moving water.

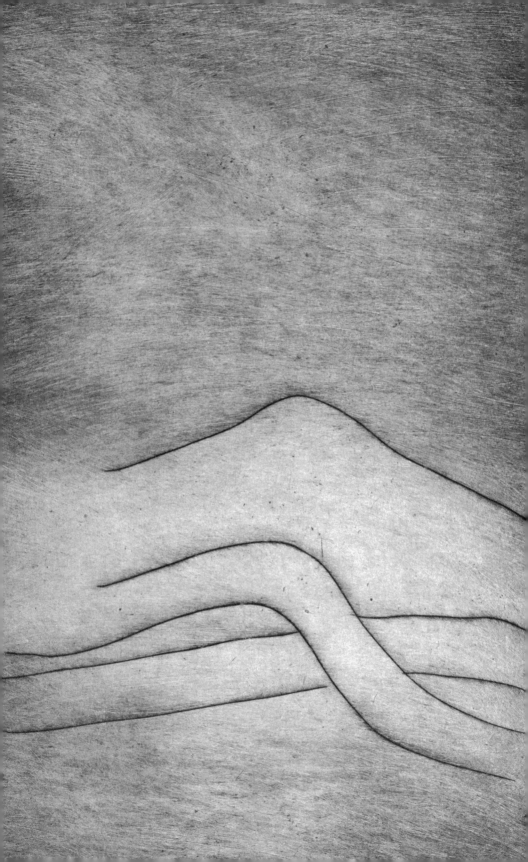

FROM THE NEW WORLD (1)

Kovařík's mother, who was an early riser, looked out her kitchen window and saw the Master walking back and forth, well before 5 a.m. the morning after the family arrived in town. She ran out to see what the trouble was. Had something happened? she cried.

In one way, no, Dvořák told her. Nothing had happened.

But in another way, he said, a great deal had happened. For the first time in eight months, he heard the birds singing. He walked back and forth along Main Street, smoking his pipe in the early light.

And yet, this in a letter he sent back home to Bohemia: "It is very strange here. Few people and a great deal of empty space."

You can almost hear the sigh. The European sigh. Back of it, the prairie strangeness, balanced on the American vastness, lonely even with birdsong.

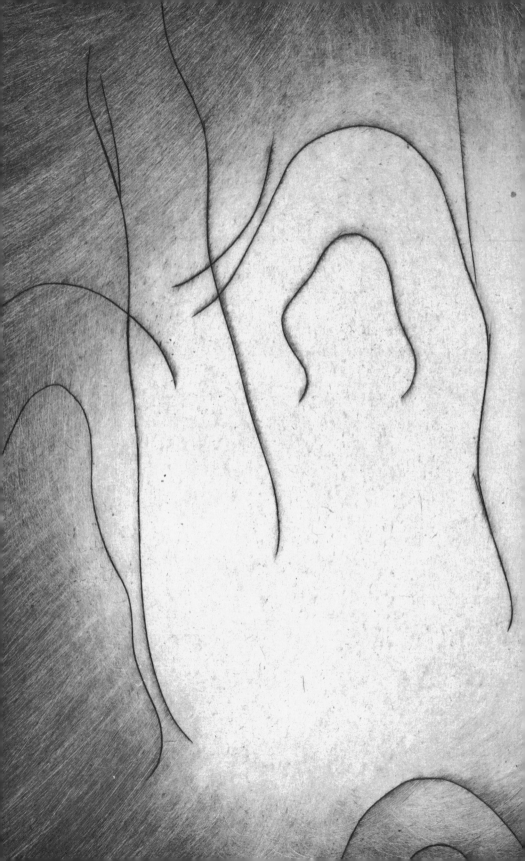

THE BELOVED

I like to think everything can be said, described. It's how I see my job, describing things. That's why I love landscape, this passing farmland, the gullies just filling with high grass, the jots of birds, the whole encouraging sweep of health that May in the Midwest appears to be.

All of it, even that girl in blue-and-white we saw waving by the lilac, is landscape. By herself, as a person, the girl could be story. But today, attached to the lilac and the farmland, she is landscape. And landscape, that vast still life, invites description, not narration. It is lyric. It has no story: it is the beloved, and asks only to be contemplated. For contemplation is, in poetic terms, love. This lyric response to the world tends toward rhapsody.

In story, in fiction, the setting may be drawn in a few brief lines, and then—on to the action, on to the trouble, please. Landscape is not the trouble, it is where the trouble happens. Story is impatient with description, and therefore with landscape's passive willingness to be framed into a picture. Think of those girlhood afternoons, flipping past the dense descriptive passages in nineteenth century novels, skimming ahead to the dialogue. Anything to get to the story—which meant the love story.

But now, passing through this spring farmland, the love of place creates a desire to pause for description. I wish to describe the lilacs. A lyric wish. As far as I can tell, I want to describe them for no reason—because they're there, as climbers are supposed to say of mountains.

Was that how it was for Dvořák? "I know that my new Symphony and also the string quartet and quintet (composed here in Spillville) would never have been written in the manner in which I have written them, had I not seen America." He bird-dogged the scarlet tanager all over the woods and meadows of Spillville, trying to get its song transcribed accurately. And it's there, chirruping through the *scherzo* of the Opus 96 string quartet. The joy of description.

Yet, Dvořák sensed the isolation here too, the *strangeness*, as he called it: "Few people, a great deal of empty space." New York may have been crowded and noisy, but Iowa was stunned with quiet as if God, at first acting like a good Czech, had made the right landscape, but then faltered, sketching in the peasants haphazardly, too faintly.

Dvořák's rhapsodic voice is not a gush of feeling. That's the common mistake, to think of Romantics as "emotional." In fact, the Romantic consciousness is bred not of feeling, but of faith. Sometimes too much faith for the contemporary sophisticated audience which prefers an edgier sound to Dvořák's swells and murmurs. Birds, wind, moving water—these form his compact with life.

No wonder Dvořák never had much luck with opera, the human drama. His only great operatic triumph is *Rusalka*, the story of a mermaid who falls in love with a human. The most beautiful aria is Rusalka's song to the moon, the pantheistic swoon of a solitary. People are walk-ons, their frantic dilemmas overwhelmed by the greater punishments and assurances of creation itself. Landscape alone is real. Landscape and its true love, the poetic consciousness, the lyric intelligence which contemplates and reiterates the created world. The Romantic.

Once Dvořák had his singing bird, his wind zinging through a wheatfield, his rushing waterfall, he was companioned—not as human beings seeking relation with other human beings are companioned, but as the soul seeking God is companioned. The scarlet tanager didn't make him *feel* good, certainly it didn't inspire love; he called it his "damn bird." But its song, fleet and difficult to capture, formed an article of his faith.

The faith, put plainly, was that God was in the song; God was even in the difficulty. And what do you do with God but serve Him? Get out the notebook and transcribe.

The chilly spaces left between people must always have remained for him, as he said, *strange*. As a Central European travelling with his family entourage, he could observe that strangeness, even be dismayed by it, without being harmed. But that loneliness was part of human feeling. Whereas, the relationship to bird, wind, rushing water was part of divine faith. Landscape and faith formed the foundation and arc that enclosed human endeavor in all its frantic loneliness. Faith didn't provide a warm, comfortable sensation (Dvořák was one of the scowling Romantics), but it gave the sense of vocation, of productive servitude, without which an artist is left to rely on the inflation of personal qualities, on "originality," on "being unique."

But what is it, now, to wish to get out the notebook and transcribe, to describe the lilacs? Where's the divinity in description?

The desire to describe the lilacs, the lyric impulse, is easily disparaged. You want a description of the lilacs? Consult the Romantic poets, go to the nineteenth century. They took care of all that. A little sentimental, but pretty.

And for God's sake, we keep warning each other these days, don't be sentimental.

THE BIG WORRY

Dvořák's sense of American strangeness stemmed from the historical fact of immigration, the recognition of loneliness implicit in the great nineteenth century European migration. And not just loneliness. He sensed as well, I think, the deeply buried *shame* of the banished. American loneliness or modern alienation, as it is called, is fundamentally the inherited sensation of banishment.

Our national myth teaches that our ancestors came here to pursue freedom (especially of religion or "thought"), but that would have been a luxurious motive for Dvořák's people. Poverty made pioneers. Poverty also made the shame of banishment, a shame which is only now, in the third and fourth generations, being redressed and reworked into a heritage. A peculiarity of the American historical sensibility allows us to be proud of great-grandfathers (or even grandfathers) who lived in crushing poverty, while the poverty of a father is too close for comfort.

The strangeness of immigration (or, as I'm thinking of it, the strangeness of banishment) that captured Dvořák's attention was an historical fact that impressed itself, literally, on the landscape: all those immigrants made the big leap from the Old World and then hunkered down for good on a patch of American soil. The strangeness was bred as much from their being so determinedly *settled* as it was from their being uprooted in the first place.

The historical fact that haunts our own times and gives us a sense of strangeness is also linked to our relation with the landscape. Our "historical fact" is the persistent threat of extinction. No place, no matter how beloved—or how remote—is safe anymore.

We cannot even join the long line of prophetic, worried Romantics who managed to locate the secure sanctity of certain untouched landscapes when they wrote their lyric poetry in the shadow of industrialism. Blake, Wordsworth, even a figure as recent as Lawrence, could keep looking for that safe place, that spot of goodness left on Earth. But now, we know we're all in it together—even if our governments rarely act that way. No amount of lyric description can love the "beautiful," the "untouched" landscape back from the bomb.

Yet I'm stuck with faith. Not faith that *it* "won't happen." And not a fatalistic belief that, what-the-hell, it will. I don't *know*—nobody does.

Rather, it's the faith that this helpless thing, lyric perception, is an authentic response to the world's impossible contradictions which seem to resolve themselves, finally, as beauty. In fact, I believe that lyricism represents a form of courage, for it is the only response as thoroughly vulnerable as the jeopardized world itself is.

Lyricism is the ancient impulse to praise, the individual cry at the perception of glory. In that, it's not far from prayer, I suppose.

The artist's work, it is sometimes said, is to celebrate. But really that is not so; it is to express wonder. And something terrible resides at the heart of wonder. Celebration is social, amenable. Wonder has a chaotic splendor. It moves into experience rather than into judgement. It zooms headlong into the act of perception where the lyric is bred of awe.

Whitman said the role of the poet is not to teach people about beauty; people can do that on their own: everyone is born lyrical. Rather, the poet's work is "to indicate the path between reality and men's souls." Which strikes me not only as a sound program for mental health but as a definition of faith.

The path between our current reality and our souls runs along a sheer fall. Do not go into this soft May farmscape, the lilacs bowing with their lavender burden, and expect to feel no pain. Expect to feel dislocation. A contemporary form of banishment. But the lyric sensation rises to meet the lilac in the ancient encounter: wonder.

Clare is next to me in the back seat, bent over a piece of

construction paper which she holds firmly against the movement of the car, drawing with a blunt crayon a picture of a girl standing in a yard, waving by a big bush. Look twice. Once for love, once for survival.

FAITH

I studied with the birds, flowers, trees, God and myself.

—DVOŘÁK

Does anyone talk that way any more? The great Romantic trust. The faithfulness of it, falling on the breast of existence, knowing it will bear you up.

I remember something like that. Lying on the grass in my grandmother's backyard years ago, wind through the apple tree. My uncle comes out of the kitchen drinking a bottle of Grain Belt. "Hi, pumpkin," he says. "Whadaya doing—listening to the grass grow?"

Yes. Yes, I am.

"You better move. One of them apples is gonna fall right on your head."

From time to time the *plonk* of a fallen apple interrupted the taffeta sound of the wind in the leaves overhead. Apples were landing all around me.

"You better move, Miss Dreamer. One of them apples. . . ."

I looked up through the knotted branches of the apple tree to the bright, winking sky. *I don't have to move. I'm lucky.*

I lay there the whole afternoon, drifting, untouched. Studying.

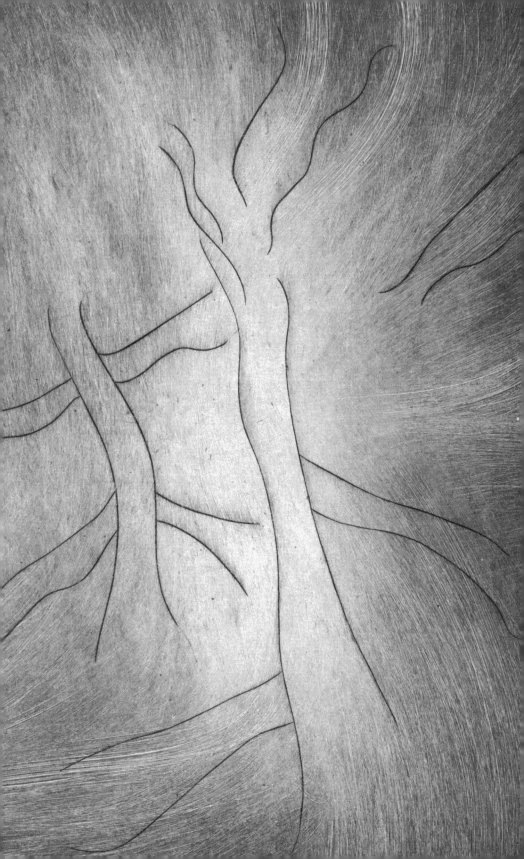

POSTCARD (1)

"A completely Czech village," Dvořák wrote home. "They have their own school, church—everything Czech. . . ."

Almost 100 years later, and we're having a cup of coffee at the Czech Inn café, which is almost empty. Clare has scrounged a couple of quarters and gone off to play the pinball machine in the corner.

Two couples of retirement age step into the big barroom, the women in the lead, husbands trailing slightly behind, one of them holding a map. The men are wearing those knit sport shirts which, though pastel, seem dun-colored.

The wives advance on the table where several fortyish men are sitting, including the owner who poured our coffee. They have coffee mugs and are smoking, leaning back in their chairs, their seed corn hats pushed back on their heads. The owner has a great moon of a belly which he displays under a tight tee shirt.

"We were wondering," the larger woman calls out before they have reached the table, "what kind of authentic Czech cuisine you have on the menu here."

The owner turns toward her, still maintaining the tilt of his chair. "Come again?" he says, eyeing her.

"We're especially interested in liver dumpling soup."

The owner says nothing. The husbands are turning toward the door.

"We just visited the museum," the smaller woman puts in. "We were thinking of goose, or roast pork and those little yellow dumplings. . . ."

"We've got the hoagies," the owner says, "which we put in the microwave." He indicates a stack of cellophane-wrapped packages behind the bar near a big aluminum coffee urn. "And we've got the Tombstones."

"Tombstones?" A quiver of fright passes across her face.

"Pizza."

"Oh," the smaller woman says gamely, "I don't believe we're in the mood for Italian."

[34]

"Come again?" he says, letting his chair down on all four legs, leaning back to his buddies.

For an instant, a crazy rage licks through me. I seek, as anger always does, a culprit—these mild women looking for what clearly is not here? The husbands with their even milder abandonment of their wives' desires? Or is my fury—yes—for the owner, his satisfaction in turning them away.

This is the anger which is Out of All Proportion. I want to yell, "Make the dumplings. You know how it's done. It's in the blood, Czech-boy."

And then I want us all to sit down and eat and eat. The rage of lost homely details, out of all proportion.

Outside, the husbands stand in the middle of the empty square, by the bandstand erected in memory of the Spillville dead from the First World War. All the soldiers' names are etched on the side, maybe twenty or thirty names. Place names of the famous battles are inscribed in the stone which runs around the top of the gazebo: Ypres, Somme, Marne, Argonne Forest, Château-Thierry. I don't recognize all the names of these places.

The men turn when they hear the Czech Inn door open. They raise their hands to shield their eyes from the sun as they watch their wives approach. The light falls full on the women's faces, exposing their paleness, making them appear drained, helpless as statues left in the open.

LILAC

We're on our way out of town now, just to see what's on the other side of it before we settle in. I stare out the car window, see the landscape seem to leave us, rather than we leave it.

There are more beloved places than I realized before when the category only included the lovely. Look at all the brutal places that have become beloved because the world happened there—terribly, irrevocably. You know the names. They ring their awful alarms, and do the only thing history seems to do. They hand on our heritage as a list of names.

What would Dvořák make of all this post-Romantic worry, he who trolled through the Spillville woods with his notebook, happy to hear the birds? I open my notebook, begin idly: *A girl about twelve, wearing a blue-and-white dress, stood waving, dwarfed by a huge lilac bush whose blossoms. . . .*

Might as well try again to describe the lilacs, that exotic Slavic flower that has taken so well to our homey Midwest. But then, the Midwest is exotic to the Slavs at home. The lilacs are of this place—and not of it. They deserve the attention. They survived the journey over. And flourished.

II
STUDIO

THE WORLD'S SMALLEST CHURCH

How simple certain places want to be. This Iowa. On the highway, the earth was ranged in rows of newly sprouted corn. The dark ceramic blue of the Harvestore silos, holding silage at a temperature that makes pigs tipsy and happy, might have been a matched canister set on a kitchen counter.

Saying a place is flat is another way of pretending it's simpler than it is. Nebraska is flat, we say. And Kansas is flat. North and South Dakota, and Iowa—flat, flat, flat. The whole Midwest is supposed to be flat. Yet here we are, Iowa, on our way to check out the World's Smallest Church (as the sign on the road promised), outside of Spillville, and it's all up and down, dips and curves.

And then, we'll go home and say, Iowa? Oh yeah, flat. Lots of corn. Really flat.

Another thing. Turning onto this doodle of a road has somehow pitched us harder into the landscape. There is no forest, but there is the sensation that now we're going deeper. The *deeper* of characters in fairy tales who set off from home and, sooner or later, must enter a deep wood.

Deeper into this mild hilliness, this food-growing, church-going place. The long grasses and reedy beginnings of tiger lilies stray over the culverts onto the edges of the road. Later in the season, people pick the black-spotted orange lily blossoms for salad. Right now, for those who know where to look, lamb's quarters are tender; they make a peppery salad. And somewhere nearby, not visible to us, but somewhere known to certain people who aren't telling, there are elm groves where under the damp leaf-mulch of last fall, the morels are beginning to emerge.

But we're not stopping, not for wildflowers, not even for wild mushrooms. We're hurtling toward that perverse superlative: the Smallest. . . .

LIGHTNING

"He used to sit over here on the hillside. . . . That's where he used to sit a lot. There was a big white oak tree there. And lightning struck it one time and split it. So I told John about it and he come down and made posts out of the trunk and out of the limbs.

"And he sawed the stump off about that high off the ground. That's where Dvořák always set, you know. Listen to bluejays.

"He used to have us chase them bluejays up to him to hear that chirp, you know. And then, when they'd leave, well, you know, he'd turn and listen to that echo from the waterfall from the dam down here."

"He used to sit there, listen to that whizzing sound coming through a timothy field. He'd listen to any kind of a noise."

". . . . Cattle coming across the river. And you know how they splash in the water. We was walking along. And boy, he stopped and listened to that splashing. Started making notes, you know.

"That was him, boy. Any noise he heard, he'd stop and listen."

THUNDER

The first morning, Dvořák walked up the hill to St. Wenceslas Church. It was the birthday of his oldest daughter, Otilka: she was fifteen. In Prague she had been eager to see *Amerika*. In New York she was homesick for Bohemia. A fickleness common, perhaps inevitable, to the pilgrim.

St. Wenceslas was—is—a big church for such a small town. An immigrant extravagance. Weekday Mass at 6 a.m. was a sleepy affair. It was attended by old women, *babičky* telling their beads while Father Bílý, remote at the front, murmured his way through the Latin, his back to the congregation of grannies.

Father Bílý was a favorite of Dvořák. All summer he allowed Otilka and the younger children to take his two ponies for rides. They went along the Turkey River, out of town, all the way to the nearby village of Protivin, free as birds.

Mrs. Dvořák, who was said to have a lovely singing voice, stayed at home most of the time in the brick house on Main Street which the family rented. She made seven pieces of lace that summer.

The Master (as the rest of the town, following Kovařík, called Dvořák, to distinguish him from the Spillville butcher, also Dvořák) rose at four, took his walk along the Turkey River, a minor tributary of the Mississippi, listening to the birds and the waterfall made by the beaver dam. Then he walked up to Mass. The summer routine. A Vysoká routine. Nights, he and Mrs. Dvořák played cards, mostly *darda*; sometimes they put together a group for chamber music.

That first morning, Otilka's birthday, no one noticed him arrive at the church. He went up the back to the choir loft, sat at the organ. Then, into the filtered light of the cool, cream-colored echo chamber lined with tall stained-glass panels, he bammed out *"Bože, před tvou velebností"* ("God Your Majesty, Before You"). A Czech hymn, known to everyone.

He let them know he was there.

By the end of the summer they were asking him after Mass

what they would be singing the next day. The boy who worked the bellows for him said the Master pulled all the stops for the postlude. The grannies walked out singing, and "the organ sounded like thunder."

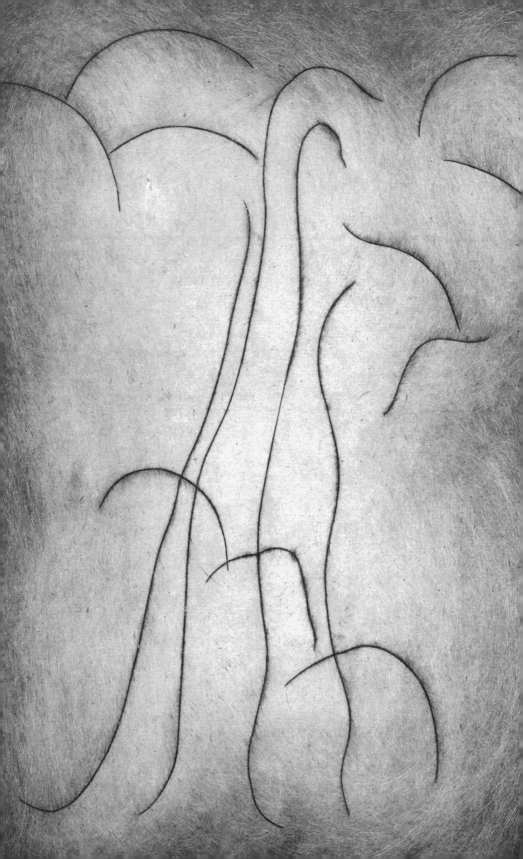

RICE

Did I expect to have to duck my head? Maybe crawl on my hands and knees to get through the tiny church doors? How small should The World's Smallest be?

Smaller than this. And yet—gather six souls, pack them along the baby-blue pews in here, and you'd have a crowd. This place isn't a miniature, not a doll church with a teeny-weeny altar, itty-bitty stained-glass window, Thumbelina pulpit. Not something you stare at, marveling at the cleverness that devised such tininess.

It's really a church. But small. OK, the smallest. Give the people of Festina, Iowa (Unincorporated) their statistic. It is small the way a small person is really a person. Small, not like a replica, but the way real things can be.

I've had this feeling before: at home one day, standing in a check-out line at the Country Club Market behind a Hmong woman, a tribal refugee from the mountains of Southeast Asia. She was wearing a child's red Keds and a Day-Glo orange jacket that would have fit an American ten-year-old. Her baby, which was not smaller than a Caucasian baby and therefore seemed very large, was lashed to her back with a woolen shawl, giving her a look of serene practicality.

She did not come up to my shoulder. I stood behind her, aware of the space I occupied. She never looked at me, not even when I inadvertently bumped her slightly with my cart. She shifted forward, as if she were the larger presence and I were invisible.

She was beautifully proportioned, thin and lithe, her minute features calibrated exactly. I registered in my American body, rather than in my thoughts—*that's the right size for a human being.* The size we ought to be.

Even my cart of groceries seemed wrong, too random, as if I had passed my big hand over the whole world, grabbing. Frozen taco shells; a carton of chicken livers I planned to do something interesting with, involving a lot of soy sauce and fresh ginger; a triangle of Brie; a bottle of kosher half-dills; the makings of manicotti.

Whereas, the small Asian woman was lifting her major purchase, a great pillowcase of rice in a cotton sack. There were other things in her cart; they all made sense, fit together as she and her sleeping baby fit together. She lifted out a spray of cilantro last, laying the feathery leaves on top of the twenty-pound sack of rice like a corsage, leaving her narrow, capable child's hand on top of the plump cotton sack as if reassuring a slumbering body within.

Her smallness felt like sanity. A rightness attended her which felt true to what it is to be a person in the world: small, terribly small in the face of everything. But even so, placing a hand gently on what nourishes.

HIS FACE

"How did he look? He didn't have much of a look. He looked like a mean devil. But he wasn't mean. Just his looks."

"We were afraid of him. He had whiskers like wires, sticking out."

"His sharp eyes looked straight through you."

"Sometimes he'd be real friendly and have a smile once in a while. But very seldom."

NAPOLEON

The garden is old, full of perennials which have made their way around The World's Smallest Church, through the graveyard in the back, along the edges of the rusted wire fence that marks the church line from the field beyond, and then around to the front and the wrought-iron gates. Masses of lily-of-the-valley fill out the lurking places to the back and side of the church, their tulip-like leaves cloaking the white bells emerging on the damp stalks.

The little church, dedicated to St. Anthony (for what reason?), was built, the bronze plaque says, in 1885 to fulfill a vow. The mother of Johann Gaertner, whoever she was, whoever he was, made one of those pacts with God: You do this, I'll do that. Deal?

Her son had been drafted into the French army by Napoleon, and she wanted him safely returned from the Russian campaign. The *War and Peace* war, Tolstoy's Prince Andrei's.

And Johann was returned. Here in the cool churchyard is his grave, with a worn granite obelisk marking his dates and his brush with history:

FOUGHT WITH

NAPOLEON

BONAPARTE

AT MOSCOW

AND WATERLOO

A red cedar is spreading its long branches over the place; the leaves whinny softly in the breeze overhead.

He lived to be a very old man, this teenager who fought with Bonaparte. Long enough to be buried far from battle, in Iowa where the name Waterloo means something else altogether.

A patch of asparagus is growing near the obelisk, left over from a kitchen garden perhaps, as if Johann's mother wanted her boy to have a reliable source of vegetables. Down from the

asparagus, closer to another grave, stands a statue marked "Our Lady of the Seven Dolors."

The statue has been slightly washed away, as if it were made of sand. But it is still possible to see the seven little swords stabbing her heart picador-style. She wears this heart like a brooch, displayed on her upper left bodice, and she gazes up to the heavens through the oak leaves. Another mother with a soldier-boy. The statue was erected, the marker says, in honor of T Sgt Cyril E. Schneberger:

BORN OLD MISSION, IOWA	1917
KILLED MANILA	1945
BURIED AT FESTINA	1949

The birds are everywhere, mad with joy, really singing, not just chirping. Whole long odes, in an abrupt Morse-code teletype. They flit from gravestone to gravestone, in and out of patches of sun and shadow. One, a brownish Harris tweed bird, lands briefly on the shoulder of the Lady of the Seven Dolors.

I step near. He's off again, racketing around, and then, up and away, out of sight.

There must be dozens of them, singing their hearts out. Ecstatic or desperate—it's hard to tell which it is. But it's music. We're right, I'm sure, to call it music.

A letter home:

"Spillville is a purely Czech settlement, founded by a certain Bavarian German Spielmann who christened the place Spillville. He died four years ago, and in the morning when I went to church my way took me past his grave.

"Strange thoughts always fill my mind at the sight of it, as of the graves of many other Czech countrymen who sleep their last sleep here. These people came to this place about forty years ago, mostly from the neighborhood of Písek, Tábor. . . . All the poorest of the poor. And after great hardships and struggle, they are very well off here. . . ."

At home, around this time of year, my father loads the backseat of his car with pots of red and white geraniums and sprengerai fern. He drives the couple of miles to Calvary Cemetery to plant the silver-painted urn in front of the graves of his father, his mother, and his only brother, Frank, who has been there the longest, alone for decades before his parents arrived. He was killed in a factory accident in his twenties.

I always wait too long to ask to go along. "Oh, I was out there last week already," my father will say. "It's all planted." And I'm disappointed.

And relieved. It's a pleasant enough place, as it is here in this little Festina graveyard. People keep up the graves, my mother says, approving. The trees there are old enough to be park-like and graceful, the grass is lush and trim, as here.

A few pine trees make a small cove for our three. The fallen pine needles turn a rich sawdust color on the ground. They

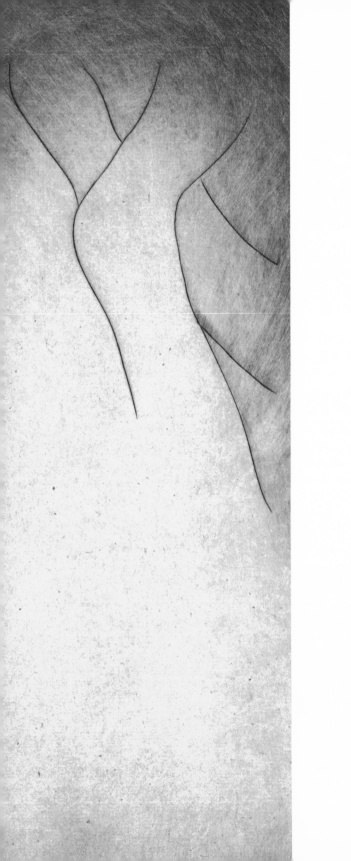

give off a sudden sharp cleansing smell when you step on them, crushing them.

But the lot is for four. Someone is missing. And I've always been badly superstitious.

"Strange thoughts always fill my mind at the sight of it, as of the graves of many other Czech countrymen who sleep their last sleep here. . . All the poorest of the poor. And after great hardships and struggle, they are very well off here. . . ."

I realize, standing in this other graveyard, I cannot tell if he meant that after great hardship the poorest of the poor triumphed in the New World over the ancestral deprivation of the Old.

Or did the Master mean: they're better off in the grave? Better given back to the earth where they rest, past hardship, beyond struggle?

It could be either. Text is mystery.

STARS

Dandelions button the dark grass back of the church. Phlox and alyssum run along the fence, and a finely-shaped columbine appears here and there like a bit of misplaced mountain flora. The iris, however, are hardly budded; they won't flower for a couple of weeks, I'd guess, and the roses are just putting out leaves. No lilacs—that surprises me. But at the front of the church doors, massy ecru flowers spill over the bridal wreath bushes.

A bride should be entering.

But such a small place has nothing to do with crowds or celebration. Nothing to do with the idea of union, either. It's all about solitude. The singular encounter. Enter alone. Meet your God.

There's no organ in here. Dvořák couldn't slip in and blast the immigrant grandmothers at silent morning Mass into shyly following the organ, singing to the Lord God Majesty in the old language.

St. Anthony is front and center with a lily in his left hand, the baby Jesus perched on a book in his right. The altar is thick with wax flowers. A sign at the side says in sharp black letters

KINDLY REFRAIN FROM TOUCHING
OBJECTS ON ALTAR

What a little white box of a place. A shrine to claustrophobia. Easy to imagine an awful key-turning-in-the-lock sound, a cackle, the clicking of shoes down the front walk: I'm shut in, abandoned to this narrow, white cabinet. The sentence, as always: to think my thoughts.

The palms of my hands bristle with dampness. I smile familiarly at claustrophobia: old friend. First met in the dark cubicle of the confessional of St. Luke's church when I was seven, the little window sliding open to receive my sins.

I look up from my place on the front baby-blue pew, the

involuntary gesture of the Lady of the Dolors out in the garden. Looking for *a way out*, not for solace and not for an explanation. I had misunderstood that expression in the garden.

The ceiling does help. It is arched, covered like the old Uptown movie theater in St. Paul with silver stars. Only, these are big, stencilled five-pointed jobs. Just a few of them, tossed on the small sky of the ceiling. They help.

But this is no place to stay long. Thoughts want fields. Cows, somewhere nearby, are giving a low honking sound like patient cars in an eternal traffic jam. The birds are out there, too, crazed with sweetness. All those flowers coming on.

Music wouldn't be possible in here. The resonance would crowd in on itself, cramming notes together, allowing no pause. Without the chance of music, is it really a church? The smallness is one thing, but no place for music is something else again.

Not a church then, a hermitage. A cell.

The (dry) holy water font at the back has been mistaken by visitors for a litter holder; several styrofoam cups are mashed into it. A little wooden holder (empty) in the vestibule reads:

TIMELY PAMPHLETS
DROP COIN IN BOX

There is no box. There are no pamphlets. No holy water.

"Go in Peace," it says, stencilled boldly over the door. That at least is right. Always a timely message.

I reach down, turn the porcelain knob of the door, and stand blinking in the sun on the front step leading to the white-water of the bridal wreath hedges. Out with the sun, with the bliss-bound birds, the soft dust of the gravel road, away from the attempt to make friends with God in that little box.

What with the opulent bridal wreath, the sweet air, the escape from the cell, I'm glad, as if something has been decided in favor of the dolorous mother, against all the usual odds. She got her boy back. Chalk one up for the humans.

Stepping forward into the sun I begin puzzling out his life. If the little church was built in 1885 (the bronze plaque says so), and if Johann, who fought with Bonaparte at Moscow and Waterloo, was born in 1793 and died in 1887 (it's on his obelisk), then it is clear how things really happened.

It was Johann himself who built the World's Smallest Church. His mother was long gone. She didn't keep her end of the bargain after all. Or rather, she didn't bargain with God— she just did what the hand-wringing mothers have always done. She wished. Hard.

Then her boy left her anyway, this time going in the other

direction, toward the New World. Did she really expect he'd hang around the old country, this teenager who fought with Bonaparte at Moscow and Waterloo?

But the church got built by Johann and his neighbors, two years before his death, when he was in his nineties. I suppose he built it to set his mother's debt right in the end.

No, too sentimental. He built it just to have a place to rest his old bones, the remains of the darling boy sent off to war. We all have to be somewhere, even when we're dead. Bury the body in the earth, scatter the ashes at sea.

There's vanity in the claustrophobia of the place. It's a mausoleum, not a chapel. That's what suffocates. The Smallest Church, built for the boy who fought for the little despot.

BACHELORS

Late afternoon. Back in Spillville, the house where the Dvořáks lived. Old brick, newly tuck-pointed, right on the main drag leading to the Turkey River where Dvořák sat on the white oak stump. The woods are a municipal park now, cleared somewhat, a big boulder with a plaque marking his favorite spot. No white oak stump, though. Take its existence on faith: the clear memory of the boy who flushed bluejays for the Master.

The brick house is a museum now. Not "The Dvořák Museum." The big gold letters on the black background say BILY CLOCKS. The first floor is devoted to the Bílý brothers, two bachelors who spent their winters carving clocks. Or more exactly, carving intricate wooden sculptures into which, almost as an afterthought, some kind of time-keeping mechanism was added.

There's a colored postcard for sale on the rack at the front counter, the aged Bílý brothers straight and rectitudinous, sitting on plain wooden chairs, their trousers hitched up by wide suspenders, their gaze guileless. No elderly twinkle, no lingering wisp of libido. Their hands are cupped in their laps like shallow bowls. Are they smiling? Are they alive or already beginning to be statuary? And—my inevitable question about the very old—can I see the person, the bundle of urges that constitutes what, in younger faces, we think of as personality?

I cannot. They are so old, balding and feather-haired and soft, they are becoming babies again to the eye.

The curious certainty we all seem to have—even the matronly guide at the front counter who sold us our tickets for the museum—that the adjective *bachelor* is necessary, explains something of the mystery of these two. What does it mean to be a bachelor, what vow has been taken?

The vow of childhood. The desire to remain loyal to the vocation of wonder. Entranced, ornamenting time in great clock-epics of wood.

But there is a world that won't be kept at bay. The Bílý brothers had that stray detail (call it adulthood) somewhere in their whittling hands. In the corner stands a replica of the Little Brown Church in the Vale which the brothers carved meticulously (from a photograph—they never went further than 35 miles from home). The little church, carved of black walnut, is dark and baleful, small as it is. A place designed for funerals.

But then, the matronly guide flicks a switch on the side of the model. A low whirr starts up, and a mechanism opens the back door, sending two identical sets of figures, two bridal couples, along a track beside the church and curving to the front where they pause a moment, making a low clicking sound, until the chapel doors open, allowing them to enter the dim interior of the church. The male figures are in black, stiff and straight; the brides are painted a flawed, grayish white.

If you bend your head and peer forward into the church, it is possible to see several rows of pews inside. Perhaps there is a tiny sanctuary and altar; I can't see for sure. But there they are, the two faded bridegrooms, very close, one behind the other, on a steady track that brings them to the marriage altar, together, as they must have understood God ordained them to be.

PROXIMITY

I must admit, standing here on the staircase leading to the second floor (where the Bílý clocks give way to Dvořák's studio), that I've never succeeded in being bored by the houses of the great. The specificity of any residence is a proof, a *here*, though the *now* is long gone. This room, right here, is where. . . .

I remember the feeling, going that first time to the Keats house in Hampstead. Not reverence. Almost fear. Proximity to the scene of genius had me rattled, and I crept around the narrow, lovely double house whose other tenants had been Fanny Brawne and her mother. Tears started foolishly to my eyes when I stood before the bedroom where he had his first hemorrhage—"I know that blood, it's arterial blood. I must die."

And 19 Berggasse in Vienna. I arrived late, just before five o'clock. No one there except the young attendant, wearing round, owlish spectacles like an intellectual of the Thirties. He kept looking at his watch.

"Where is the couch?" I asked.

There wasn't a stick of furniture in the place, just blow-ups of photographs on the walls, showing the suffocating Victorian decorations of yesteryear that once filled the flat.

"The couch is not in residence," he said stiffly, as of a person. "It is with Anna Freud in London."

The place did not have the look of a legitimate museum. It looked as if a band of loyalists managed to get the rent paid and keep the floor swept. Standing in that bare room, I felt the world's hostility, its injunction against news from the deep personal interior. Freud was still an outcast, hardly the father of anything at all. Still a madman who talked about the dirty thoughts of children. A Jew run out of town in the end, the swastika hoisted over his door.

The young man stood by the door, and said, "Please," making a slight motion with his feet, just shy of heel-clicking. He locked up, and flew down the stairs ahead of me like the rabbit in *Alice*, actually saying distractedly as he went, "I'm late, very late for . . ."

I followed slowly by myself. I paused at a turn in the stone stairway leading down to the inner courtyard. Suddenly, as surely as if it were a fact, I knew that this turn, this spot right here, was where many before me had stopped, struck.

I had located the brief instant between the horizontal world of the couch and the vertical life of the street. The clarifying instant alone after the baffling code of the dream had yielded to the Professor. I felt it physically. My hand touched the rough gray stone of the balustrade.

But what, really, had I seen up there? A couple of empty rooms with big black and white photos of Victorian comfort, which looked to me like bad taste.

And this instant on the stone staircase leading down from the consulting room to the courtyard and the street. That pause made a bridge to the other side of time. I went across its frail span and was there with him.

LABOR

Up the narrow stairway on the second floor. The small side bedroom off from the front master bedroom. This must be the studio. The room where the Master composed. He finished the whole sketch of the Opus 96 quartet, the *American*, the first three days in the house. It remains his most beloved with audiences, though critics sometimes fault it for its breezy, impressionistic personality.

"Thanks to the Lord God," Dvořák wrote after the last bar of the sketch. "I am satisfied, it went very quickly." He marked the moment: 6 p.m., June 10, 1893.

Like a woman talking about her safe labor and delivery, right down to the minute. It went quickly. Thank God. A live birth.

A spinet organ, so unobtrusive it looks more like a sideboard than an instrument, is set along one wall of the studio. A soiled but neatly lettered sign, propped on the yellowed keyboard, reads, "This organ played by Antonín Dvořák, Spillville, 1893." The other walls are crowded with display cases.

Selected inventory, books: *The World of Today; Wonders of the Past; Forty Famous Ships; Reptiles of the World; The Story of Our Civilization* (3 vols.).

A whole shelf devoted to clocks: *The Book of American Clocks; Time and Timekeepers; Old Scottish Clockmakers 1453–1850; Chats on Old Clocks.*

A shelf labelled "Practical Affairs": *Common Sense Stair Building and Hand Railing; The Boy Mechanic.* And, tucked between *A History of Architecture* and *Practical Bungalows and Cottages,* a pale flesh-colored book by a man named Horton, titled, *What Men Don't Like About Women.*

A travel section: *Meet the Japanese; This Is Russia; Seeing Italy; Seeing Germany* (etc.); *The Maryknoll Book of Peoples.*

The matched sets of books: Shakespeare in green and gold; an art history series in red; *The Story of Money; The Male Hormone; Copernicus and His World.* A whole case full of prayer-books, some in English, some in Czech.

Selected inventory, objects: seashells (hundreds, labelled on calling cards in a spidery hand); a bevy of porcelain thimbles painted by hand; a pair of wizened white leather gloves, elbow length. Part of a blackened ring with this faded note: "Wedding Ring. The other part lost when splitting wood."

Some sheet music of Dvořák. Next to it a 3-D picture of astronauts placing the American flag on the moon, planet earth rising moon-like itself, in the depth of the blue background.

Several objects difficult to identify, labelled "Petrified Worms from Ocean." A small constellation of fans; a wall full of china dolls; a cigar cutter; a rhinoceros tooth; an elk tooth ("from

Gerald Sharp"); and an unidentified tooth of impressive size.

All by itself, a small piece of what appears to be driftwood. But no, the note by its side reads:

National Relic
A PIECE OF ELM TREE UNDER
WHICH GEO. WASHINGTON
TOOK COMMAND OF THE
AMERICAN ARMY JULY 3, 1773

Dark Bohemian garnets in a blue velvet box: "Anna Novak Kacer wear this pin and earrings 73 years ago." No date.

A sign next to several gray objects resembling small guitar picks or blackened finger nails: "Rattle Snake Fangs from the Rattlesnake Products Company, Coral Gables, Fl."

I move from case to case, forgetting Dvořák, carried on the pure wave of eccentricity. This is the human mind displaying itself, revealing its central capacity which turns out to be not curiosity, after all, but avidity.

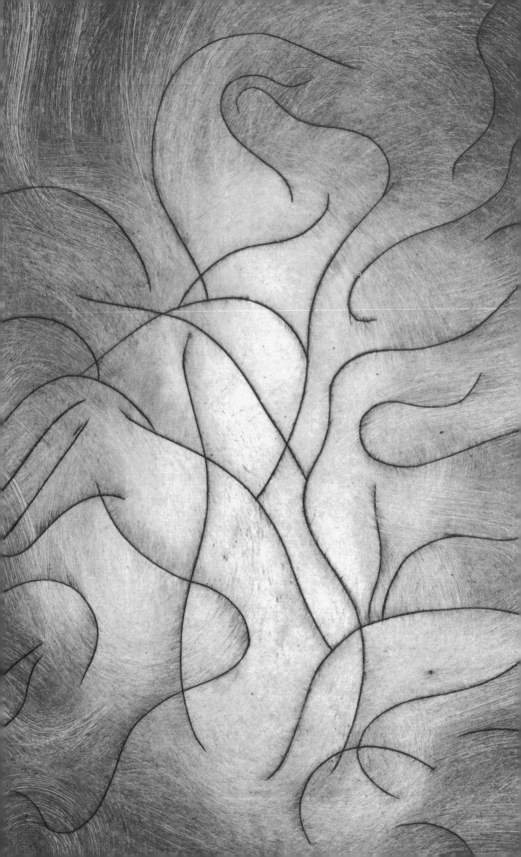

BROADSIDE

Above the little spinet organ in Dvořák's studio, someone has placed a sign, some sort of instruction. Or perhaps it is meant to be taken as a manifesto:

ART IS ACT. ARTS ARE FINE AND MECHANICAL.
The former are Architecture, Sculpture, Painting, Poetry, Music, Oratory. The latter are Agriculture, Manufacture, Mining, Transportation, Carpentry.

FINE ARTS
appeal to the imagination and
express the beautiful, the
grand, the true, the
ennobling, the inspiring.

MECHANICAL ARTS
appeal to the practical and
express the needful, the
serviceable, the mechanical,
the useful, the practical.

PIANO LESSON

When I see a piano, or even a keyboard like this spinet organ's yellowish one, I think of the room where I took my piano lessons, my own first studio.

Sister Mary Louis, my piano teacher, usually was not in the studio when I arrived for my lesson on Saturday morning. I waited alone in the pleasantly untidy room at the top of the convent school until she came billowing down the corridor from the cloister side, rolling her heavy sleeves up over the tight inner sleeve as she hurried toward me.

Her habit gave Sister a look of generality rather than specificity. It was not clear exactly what space she occupied, or what parts of her body occupied what exact territory under the black tarp. Well, not thin. Not young. And not intimate—intimacy doesn't make a good teacher. She let a person alone. Even when she took my hand, knotted like an arthritic's in a badly fingered chord, and firmly unkinked the joints, laying my fingers over the keyboard in a sensible pattern—even as she touched me, she was remote in a way that I recognized was trustworthy.

Sister had hopes of "training my ear." Wistful phrase. But I possessed the implacable will of a fantasist; no part of me, not ear, not eye, could be trained. "You've got the change in tempi!" she would exult as I geared down from a desperate *presto* to the rough canter of *allegro*.

But it was all luck, all mood. I never played a piece the same way twice. "You had it last week," she would say, mystified. "You must have lost it somewhere along the way."

It pained her that I didn't practice. She had no talent for rage; her only weapon against my sloth was hopefulness. Her moist eyes, enlarged behind her glasses and rather protruding, radiated perpetual concern. She took off the rimless glasses, polishing the lenses for long, abstracted moments while she reminded me regretfully of the benefits of the Czerny exercises.

She urged me to turn over a new leaf. For some reason, I didn't understand that she was speaking metaphorically. I puzzled over what possible good it would do to turn over a leaf and inspect its underside. And what was a *new* leaf—some dwarfish thing, tangled in the bud?

Like my parents who sent me to the convent on these Saturdays "for music" as if for a cup of sugar, Sister seemed to think of music as a parcel that could be lost or found. She was firmly on the side of discipline, but even for her the notion that music could be a source of passion was too rich for the blood. My performance highs indicated an extremism that must not be encouraged.

Or maybe she saw at a glance that I was a talentless, ordinary girl. She let me crash away, no harm done. She was too kind or too aloof in her own talent (which was genuine, I think) to hold out false hope. She never said anything enthusiastic about my playing, though at home I could wring the hearts of my mother and father who were amazed by the fiery-eyed Liszt with the heavy foot on the damper pedal in their living room.

Sister, however, played even the most complex sheet music with ease. No fireworks, no bending or straining over the keyboard. She sat square on the bench, her undefined body still under the black wrap. Her pale, doughy hands with the spatulate fingers tooled their way over the keyboard. The whole operation seemed remote, as if her hands were on automatic pilot and she was just sitting there to flip the switch to get them going.

"That was beautiful," I would say, really awed, when she finished a flawless, if curiously bland, rendition of a Chopin mazurka. I was impressed by the passionlessness of her playing. The instrument conveyed the truth of music: deep within the piano's bulging wood hip resided a wiry soul that cared nothing at all about animal emotion. Like an accountant, it looked at the bottom line; it read the numbers.

Part of the ear training involved listening to records. Sister was partial to the monaural recordings of Walter Gieseking. Oar in, oar out, through the silky waters of the Impressionists.

Debussy led Sister's charts in that category. Ravel and Saint-Saëns were right up there too. She tick-tocked the meticulous timing of Walter Gieseking like a great human metronome, standing before me, bending to left and to right as I lurched along. "Count first, dear," she urged. "*Then* work on feeling."

Feeling was fine, feeling was indispensable—she granted that. Nothing wrong with feeling. But—this was her point—I *had* feeling. No need to work further on feeling.

Besides, she would say gently, always a reluctant corrector, there was no work to feeling. And music was work.

LORE (MRS. BENDA)

Reported by many: Dvořák carried a black notebook on his walks. He marked down the sounds he heard: birds, wind, moving water. The scarlet tanager in the *scherzo* of the *American* quartet, Minnehaha's waterfall in the slow movement of the little Sonatina for Violin he wrote for Otilka and Toník.

If he forgot the notebook or if it was already full of sketches and notations, he would resort to his cuffs and pencil music on them or on the stiff front of his shirt, known as a starched bosom.

Mrs. Benda, the laundry woman of Spillville, said she had a terrible time of it, trying to get those pencil marks out.

Old Lady Benda. That was what she was called. In later years, she further obliged the story, saying she should have been smart: should have hung on to those shirts. Might have made some money off them. Old Lady Benda, the starched bosom heiress.

People like to tell this story (which isn't, come to think of it, a story). We've heard it several times already. In some versions, they do away with the black notebook altogether, and he's scribbling on his cuffs and chest as a matter of course, coming home with symphonies on his linens, given to him by the birds and the water thrumming over the millwheel in the river.

We love to believe it's simple. And it is. Afterwards.

WINDOW

Here's a curious detail. Though I loved Sister Mary Louis's studio, especially the nice confusion between living room and classroom it provided with its stacks of sheet music, the two pianos, the red mohair sofa along one wall and the claw-foot marble-top table on which rested an aquarium of sluggish goldfish—still, the real draw of the room was not its furniture or the music made there. It was the oblong window that looked out of it.

That window, placed high and oddly, without any view but sky, was the point of the room, not its boundary, but its psychological center. It reminded me of St. Valentine's window, which I'd seen in a children's book of saints. I must have seen the picture when I was very small, probably before I could read.

St. Valentine's cell was a real prison cell. I had learned that as part of the story. He was one of the remote saints tormented by the Romans—or is he one of those they've decided now never existed at all? The picture in the book showed him in monk's habit, seated at a plain table, using a plume quill to write on scraps of white paper which were lifted by white doves between the bars of the cell's window.

Small red hearts were stamped, presumably with sealing wax, on the fold of the paper. Valentine looked happy, penning away. The doves looked happy too, like elves. One was on the desk, dipping to grasp a note in the golden clothespin of his beak. Another was deftly negotiating the bars, white note angled upward. Several others, white jots against the blue, were soaring on their distant postal rounds.

Valentine seemed busy about his business, a shut-in who makes a decent living addressing envelopes from his own dining room table. The window did not concern him. It was well over his head, out of range. He was the contented convict, sending his letters to the free, but melancholy, world. The tradition was that

Valentine, who was the prisoner, wrote to cheer up everybody outside who was free. Nice paradox, not lost on me.

In November, Sister and I looked out on the tops of trees, their leafless branches creaking and swaying in the wind. Some of the top dormers of the big Victorian buildings in the neighborhood were visible, but mostly the view was sky, filled with clouds that wheeled by at great velocity.

Although it was called the studio, I was under the impression that the room had once been a nun's cell. It was at the end of a narrow corridor of tiny rooms, each filled now with a piano, rooms that had been bedrooms for students when the school had taken boarders. The studio was larger; it had two pianos, various tables cluttered with sheet music and busts of composers. It had been the room where the nun supervising the dormitory had slept. I don't know where I got this fact. Maybe—long ago—I made it up. Yet, it is also true, the way things that have taken up permanent residence in your mind are true.

I sat in the studio waiting, often a long time, staring out of the high window into the wild sky, as if into a blinded face. I wanted to live in such a room. It seemed full of purpose.

The sensation of comfort, if that's what it was, did not come from the furniture; a grand piano is a cumbersome object, and in a small room it looks pent up. No paintings on the walls, either. No color. Even the busts of Schumann and Chopin (and Dvořák? He might have been there: the Romantics were Sister's heroes) were of a cold white stone. They looked made of salt; the names were stamped in gold at the pedestal base, as on a gravemarker.

The studio, perched at the top of the heavy red brick building, seemed detachable, like a nest in a great tree that might be dislodged, blown aloft and far away.

It wasn't a disquieting thought. In fact, it was a wish. Always longing to be elsewhere, beyond the current window. A Romantic wish, convinced that the world, the real and glamorous and serious world, couldn't possibly be right here. Even the window-glass, rattling in its sash from the wind, seemed to be trying to free itself. Perhaps sitting alone there, I grasped the power of the studio—or was grasped by it.

Anyway, I believed (it was an intuition) that unlike other rooms, this room, the artist's, didn't just confine you. It released you.

III
THE FALLS

PARADISE

The Apostle Clock, The Lindbergh Clock, Parade of Nations Clock, Dvořák Clock (quite small, by Bílý standards, in the shape of a violin, the Master's face etched faintly over the fretwork), The Travel Clock, The Statuary Clock (filled with statuettes of Bílý heroes, including Dvořák, Masaryk, Ibsen, Lincoln, U.S. Grant, both Roosevelts, Immanuel Kant, Michelangelo, Thomas Edison, Shakespeare and J.J. Haug, the Spillville postmaster. All men, except a single bonneted figure marked "Pioneer Women.")

And my favorite, the Paradise Clock. God's hand, at the base, is creating sun and moon. Above that, Adam and Eve stand, looking rather nonplussed; the angel, dressed like an Indian, guards paradise at the side. Adam and Eve are wearing get-ups that look like playsuits, made of maple leaves. Eve holds a rock above her head which she appears about to pitch. But no, of course: that's the apple.

The sturdily corsetted guide leads us past each clock, the tapeloop of her speech running without pause.

There is a highpoint, a climax, though. She turns away from the clocks to tell us a story. Henry Ford, himself, the real and first Henry Ford, made overtures (her word) to the Bílý brothers upon hearing of their clocks. He had his eye on the Pioneer History clock. It is not known whether Mr. Ford himself, in person, actually came to Spillville. But it is known that he somehow got wind of the clocks, so to speak. Photographs, no doubt.

Now. Mr. Ford himself in a letter (which is somehow not available though it exists or did, at one time, certainly exist) made a firm offer to the Bílý brothers, Frank and Joseph, for the purchase of the clock. The price?

We all look at the clock. It looks like a giant, decorated armoire.

"One million dollars."

She lets us whistle through our teeth on that one. The clock is looking great.

"And though it is hard to believe, the brothers categorically turned down the offer. They would not part with a single clock. And so today, all the clocks are housed together, as the brothers wished and planned, in one house. Forever."

Together, forever. Ah yes, a Bílý dream.

I felt—I shared—the civic pride. Mrs. Benda was a chump like the rest of us. Didn't take advantage of her chances, missed the big opportunity. But the Bílýs are a different order of business.

They avoided being millionaires. *Refused* to be millionaires. Too bad, Mr. Ford. You can ask, you can plead. Your money will get you nowhere here.

This is Paradise where time stands as a statue. You hardly notice its passing. Time is all time. We're together forever, all of us, everything that ever happened. We'll never be parted. Don't be afraid. Nobody dies here.

THE KINGDOM

"The Americans expect great things of me. And the main thing is, so they say, to show them to the promised land and kingdom of a new and independent art. In short, to create a national music. Now, if the small Czech nation can have such musicians, they say, why could not they, too, when their country and people are so immense?"

He believed the answer lay in the music of the slaves, Negro spirituals, and in American Indian music, especially its insistent, patient rhythms. And, as always, as everywhere, the birds, wind, moving water. This was how he'd done it in Bohemia: go to nature, go to the people. He was a peasant, had apprenticed first as a butcher, following his father, until his talent for music somehow commanded him. He was taken to study at the choir school in the cart his father used for market.

Maybe he could not perceive the American hesitation. In the old country "the peasants" were himself, his family. His people. In America there was a boundary. Black and white, red and white. We call it racism. He stepped over the line easily, perhaps thinking Indian drum beats were as accessible to white American composers as Czech folk music was to him. He didn't hear the heavier hit of the drum on the ear, the black wail it is impossible to borrow.

POSTCARD (2)

Here's how I see them. The older boys, Otakar and Toník, swimming in the Turkey River down by the dam (washed away years ago). Mrs. Dvořák bent over her lace—probably in the front room upstairs which is full of light.

Otilka is riding Father Bílý's pony bareback. There's no evidence that she rode without a saddle, but I always see her clutching the horse's tufted mane, gripping its barrel sides with her knees.

I don't make things up on purpose; it's the desire for accuracy that causes me to see these details.

And the Master? Strangely enough, not alone. He's playing the violin with his faithful shadow, young Kovařík. And then they stop: "He'd drink a beer, eat rye bread, put salt on it. That would be his lunch. That was the real rye. You can't get that flour any more. You used to take it down here to the mill and get it ground. . . ."

"And beer? Every third house was a saloon."

INVENTORY

First of all, what Dvořák *didn't* compose here: the Symphony in D, known as the symphony *From the New World*. It was already composed when he came to Spillville, though some of the parts still needed to be copied.

The two major works begun and finished in Spillville were the *American* quartet (Opus 96) and the piano quintet (Opus 97).

And then, more tantalizing for conjecture, there are the ideas and impressions, the scribbles on the cuffs he came away with and used later.

"That's how the 'Humoresque'—the famous one—came about." The voice of an old woman. A lovely voice, modest and courteous, carrying information. Anna Kovařík, the younger sister of Josef, still alive in 1968 when two musicologists came to Spillville to interview her. The tapes are in the Minnesota Historical Society where I sit, headphones on, listening to her graceful voice, the English rounded in a pretty way by a slight Czech accent.

"He didn't write it there, as they claimed at first. No, but he had this theme. This theme occurred to him there, along the banks of the Turkey River. He worked out the ideas back in Europe in 1897."

The most famous Dvořák melody, more beloved, more known, than any of his themes. I can draw it to mind, hum it by heart, just sitting here.

FLOATS

We're drinking beer at a shaded picnic table in the park, Dvořák's big commemorative boulder off to the side, the faint rush of the Turkey River past that, down a gentle embankment. Overhead, the leaves are shushing. Contentment, not much reason to talk. Further away, past the water pump, Clare is swinging, allowing her feet to drag in the dusty depression below the swing.

Out of the peace, the clear voice of dreaminess. "Know what I'd like right now?"

We don't reply, don't even bother to look over to where he has thrown himself on the dark grass and is staring into the leafy sky. He'll go on: don't interrupt the dreamer.

"I'd like to go to one of those drive-ins, the old kind, like Porky's. You drive in there, you roll down the window and you give your order to a sixteen-year-old with a hickey on her neck."

"Cheeseburger, french fries, root beer float," I say.

"She's wearing bobby socks. They rolled them down, way down, past the ankle bone. Nobody does that anymore." The sadness of a very old man in that voice.

"And it meant something if they wore their scarves knotted on their chins."

"We used to order the basket of onion rings too. We always had onion rings."

"I could handle that."

"Right now."

"Right now."

Nobody moves. On the swing, Clare is pumping hard, going high, her legs out straight and then bent tight back. Her black hair, the color of her mother's, streams behind her when she goes forward.

"Watch me!" she's yelling. Her voice comes high and sharp on the wind. "Everybody, watch me! Catch me if I fall. I'm going higher than anybody ever in the world!"

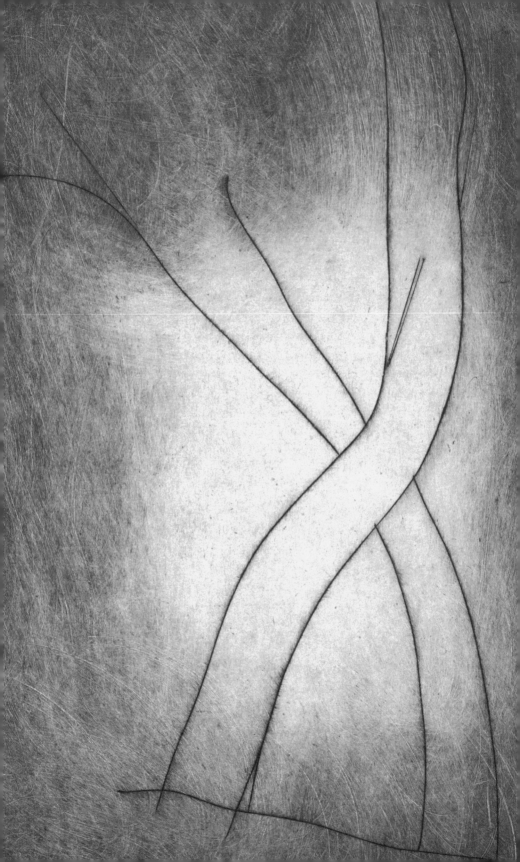

BREVITY

He was a taciturn man. One day, during a summer stay at Vysoká, he took a walk with a violinist friend who was visiting him from the city. Their way took them through the lovely countryside and then past a marshy glade. It was a hot day. The violinist complained, in passing, about the mosquitoes, slapping his bare arms.

Dvořák said nothing, kept walking.

Two days later, they happened again to take this same walk. They were going along in the usual odd silence Dvořák evoked in his companions, when they came again to the marshy glade.

"It's from the water," he said.

ARROWS

Toward the end of the summer, a small band of Kickapoo Indians came to Spillville to sell medicinal herbs. They stayed several weeks. There was a show every night—dancing, music, the sale of snake oil and Sagwar blood medicine (good for headaches and much else). There was a minstrel show as well, several blacks playing banjos and guitars, singing.

Dvořák went every night. He even had the snake oil headache treatment, administered by Big Moon, the leader of the Kickapoos. An Indian drum rhythm appears in the *scherzo* of the E flat Quintet.

Big Moon was a handsome man (there are pictures). He made arrows out of ironwood; one of them was five feet long. Big Moon, the arrow-maker. The children of the town, who flushed bluejays and scarlet tanagers for the Master, and worked the bellows of the organ and sometimes acted as interpreters ("he didn't talk English so good"), stood by and watched the launch of Big Moon's great five-foot arrow.

"How far did it go? That arrow shot from the bridge to Bolik's blacksmith shop. A block and a half. He was a good-looking Indian. Big Moon."

LAUGHING WATER

Dvořák didn't like interrupting his stay in Spillville. The place suited him. But there were invitations. To Chicago to see the World's Fair; Otilka and another of his daughters went with him there. To Omaha and to St. Paul. On this trip he left the children behind and travelled with Mrs. Dvořák.

From St. Paul, where the large Czech community gave him a bigger welcome than he really wanted, he took a buggy ride over to Minneapolis to stand by the real object of his trip, the Falls of Minnehaha. "It is so intensely beautiful that words cannot describe it," he wrote home.

He wanted to write an opera based on Longfellow's *The Song of Hiawatha*. He had read the poem in translation. Naturally, its admiration for the indigenous culture appealed to Dvořák. So did Longfellow's lyrical, if rather didactic, restatement of landscape and the beauties of nature. Dvořák never found a good libretto, and the project fizzled. He stood by the falls, asked Kovařík for a pencil (nobody had any paper), and wrote something on his cuffs. It was the theme for the Sonatina, Opus 100, a piece he wrote later, after he left Spillville.

Dvořák loved the gash in the landscape, the great outpouring a waterfall is, and on the way back to New York the family stopped at Niagara where, of course, he was even more impressed than by the decorous Minnehaha, Laughing Water.

He wanted those big, bellowy sounds, too, not just the small voices of birds, the spirit whoosh of wind. He used to stand outside the train station in Prague and is said to have known the time of each train and, what is more unusual, the number of every locomotive. To his ear, each engine had a distinct tone. Engines, the sound of them, their big, pounding hearts. Get it down on the cuffs.

He left St. Paul and returned with his wife to Spillville where their children were waiting. The medicine show was still there. It was September 7, the day before his birthday.

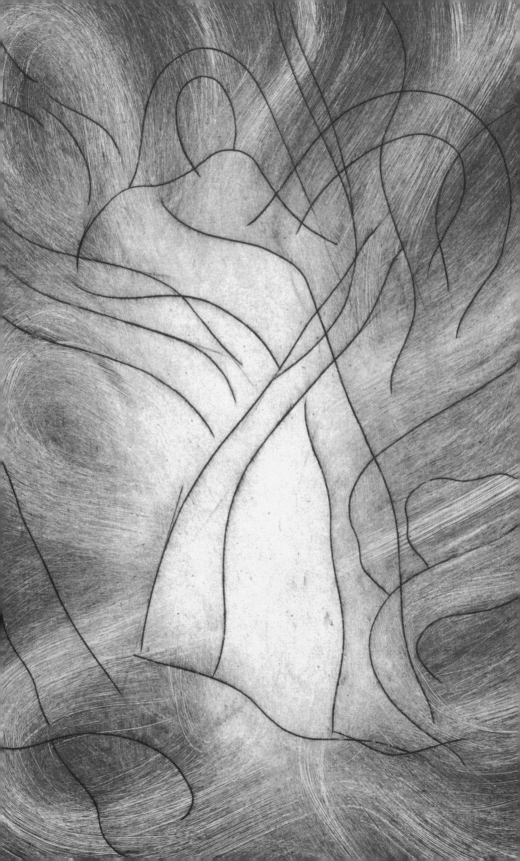

BIG MOON

Otilka rode Father Bílý's ponies all that summer. Maybe her ride took her past the Indian camp down by the river. It wasn't far from where her father walked, listening to the birds and the sound of the rushing water by the dam. Or maybe she too went in the evenings to the medicine show.

Anyway, in time she was seen, roaming around the woods, Big Moon by her side. Keeping company.

Other people say it was Kovařík who caused the trouble.

But, among those who mention it at all, the clear memory is of Big Moon. It was Big Moon with her in the woods by the Turkey River, and what of it?

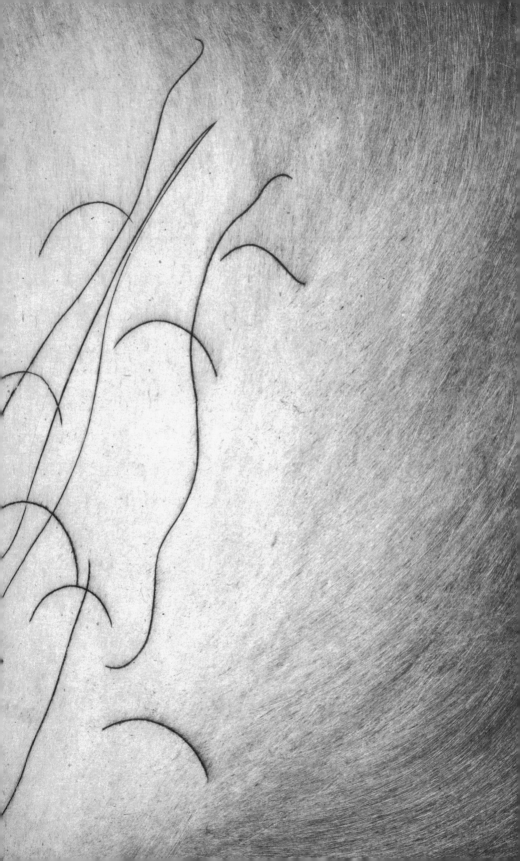

DEPARTURE

In the end, there was a betrayal. Maybe it was a form of protection, a neighborly concern. Like so much, it depends on your attitude, your place in the story. Old Lady Shima, who lived not far from the woods where Otilka and Big Moon were seen roaming together, went to Mrs. Dvořák. She told her to watch her daughter.

That night the Dvořáks started packing. They were gone the next day.

I sit at the tape machine in the State Historical Society library, headphones on, listening to the taped interview of the old man telling about it. He was one of Dvořák's boys, flushing birds, pumping the bellows. Frank Kapler (he spells it out for the interviewer: "That's K-a-p-l-e-r"). He was thirteen when Dvořák was in Spillville, eighty-five at the time of the interview, a retired steelworker. He'd be dead now, no doubt.

But I don't know: that's a firm voice. No hesitation or waver. It is deep with an attractive certainty, sounding as if the voice—clarion, undeflected—had claimed the acuity of his eyesight. He doesn't sound like a spinner of yarns. He's the one who said, "He used to sit there, listen to that whizzing sound coming through a timothy field." A detail man.

He's saying that Old Lady Shima tattled on Otilka. The family would have stayed a few weeks longer otherwise.

Frank Kapler's father, who had a three-seated buggy big enough to transport the whole family, took them early the next morning over to Calmar, to the railroad station. The same place they had arrived three months before.

Joe Mashek's father took the trunks, three or four big ones, in a different buggy.

"I and Jim Kohout, Old Lady Benda and a few others, we stood down there and waved good-bye when they made the turn there, going to Calmar."

Old Lady Shima stayed in her woods, apparently, in the way of snitches—a nose keen for love's occult odor.

MINNEHAHA

No other word of Big Moon, the arrow-maker who danced for Dvořák and cured his headache. Later Dvořák dedicated the Sonatina, Opus 100, to Otilka and Toník. The themes he used in the Sonatina were the ones that never got used in the opera he wanted to write about Longfellow's Minnehaha, the arrow-maker's daughter:

> *In the land of the Dacotahs,*
> *Where the Falls of Minnehaha*
> *Flash and gleam among the oak-trees,*
> *Laugh and leap into the valley,*
>   *There the ancient Arrow-maker*
> *Made his arrow-heads of sandstone,*
> *Arrow-heads of flint and jasper,*
> *Smoothed and sharpened at the edges,*
> *Hard and polished, keen and costly.*
>   *With him dwelt his dark-eyed daughter,*
> *Wayward as the Minnehaha,*
> *With her moods of shade and sunshine,*
> *Eyes that smiled and frowned alternate,*
> *Feet as rapid as the river,*
> *Tresses flowing like the water,*
> *And as musical a laughter:*
> *And he named her from the river,*
> *From the water-fall he named her,*
> *Minnehaha, Laughing Water.*

Five years later, in 1898, on the date of her parents' silver wedding anniversary, Otilka married Josef Suk, Dvořák's prize composition student, who became a well-known composer himself.

They were famously happy, by all accounts. In 1903 there was a baby. Then, in 1904, Dvořák died, at the age of sixty-five. Just as well.

The following year Otilka died suddenly. She was twenty-seven. Her husband, they say, went almost mad. The sadness and bleakness of his music in the following years point to his grief. He did not marry again.

THE WAVE

There's nothing in the biographies of Big Moon and the sudden departure from Spillville. It's all from Frank Kapler on this tape I first heard on the radio and play again and again on the tape recorder. Some crony of his sits in the background and occasionally makes a clucking noise, sounding like a device designed to emit approval.

Then the friend says, "Or some say she was in love with Kovařík."

Kapler, that boulder of a voice, comes on sure as a stone tossed in still water: "That may be. But she was with Big Moon. That I know."

And Old Lady Shima ran to Old Lady Dvořák. Told her to watch her daughter.

And they began packing in the night.

Of course she was in love with Kovařík. With Kovařík, with Big Moon, with Father Bílý (he wasn't old), with all of them. A girl who begged her father to take them to *Amerika*—and then pined for Bohemia in New York. That summer she was in love with love—as people describe passion in an effort to domesticate it. The real passion, not "for" someone. But the brief season when the exultant fact of existence courses madly through you.

A hot harvest morning. She rose early. The field corn was heavy and tasselled, the soybeans dense, so green they gave off a blue aura in the steamy light. Her skirt was dew-drenched to the knees by the time she walked the distance to the barn where Father Bílý stabled his ponies. She carried three little sour apples in her pockets. She pressed one against the pony's soft purplish lips; he released the clench of his jaw and took it, like a potentate allowing himself to be fed a grape. And nosed against her for more. But the other two apples remained tantalizingly hidden, in her pocket.

On their way up the hill to early morning Mass, her father and the priest saw her ride off in the blue-gold light. She flashed across the fields to Protivin on the pretty beast, dipping back

Northfield Public Library
87-3550
Northfield, MN 55057

along the Turkey River where the sun had to fight its way in broken pieces through the cottonwoods and willows along the banks. There she allowed the pony to drink.

Let her ride bareback. Let her be free. She's an American girl—for the summer, anyway.

Besides Old Lady Shima, one other person is alert. Young Kovařík, having just polished his spectacles, stands by his upstairs window. He notes the direction she takes, bent low to the pony's shaggy ear, as if confiding in him. Kovařík knows who, in that direction, can find the white mallow and many other elusive plants and edible berries along the river bank.

Certain rock-hard desires are not satisfied by faithful servitude. The Master, being a genius and the father of the lovely girl, can give Kovařík, finally, nothing. Or he gives the only thing he can: the opportunity to be of use. Which he is. The indispensable, faithful Kovařík.

He even laughed easily the day she threw herself on a springy alfalfa bed, spreading her arms like a child making an angel in the snow, and asked with that willful innocence, "Do you know what it is to be in love, Mr. Kovařík?" She stared up at those lumbering white clouds; her voice stripped him of any role.

Testing her powers. She turned to him where he sat (a proper way off, on an outcropping of rock), shading her eyes, to see the effect of her question. And then, satisfied by something she perceived in his face, she turned away again, content as if she had yanked a mallow from the bank of the river. Testing—herself, not him.

Some say she was in love with Kovařík.

That may be. But she was with Big Moon. That I know.

That voice, a mean voice—as Frank Kapler said of Dvořák's face. But not mean. He saw certain things, and now they reside in his voice. I believe the voice.

I see the rest. Girl on a pony, gold light in the blue morning sky, a glade where a good-looking man, native to the place, puts his hand surely between two clumps of fern to expose for her the white wood mallow, a plant she had never seen before.

The last thing Frank Kapler saw: his father in the three-seated buggy, turning the last turn toward Calmar, all the Dvořáks in the buggy seats. He stood there waving and waving—he and his pals, Old Lady Benda, the washerwoman, and some others. Waving good-bye for good.

MOVING WATER

Twilight, MacGregor, Iowa. We've left Spillville, headed home, working our way up the Mississippi. It is a smooth plain of water, as if it had flooded the land. I'm still used to the narrow corridor of the river further north.

The flow is stately, and the light of sunset plays on the arrays of water made by the current. It doesn't look swift, but that's a trick played on the eye. A whole tree, its spring leaves still unfurling, floats by.

In the half-light, the pale leaves of the Russian olive, planted along the main street of town, look made of frost. People are eating dinner in the nearby restaurants: whole breaded catfish is the special at most places, salad bar, baked potato in silver foil. The main street is full of antique shops, all closed now. The nineteenth century in tall brick storefronts.

"And so it is very wild here," Dvořák wrote home shortly before he left Spillville. "And sometimes very sad. Sad to despair. But habit is everything."

We get used to the way we live, the way we must live—I suppose that's what he meant. But despair—do people get used to that?

He could afford to see the "few people and a great deal of empty space" as foreign, to wonder at the alien, lonely sensation. To shiver and depart. But for us? This strangeness *is* home. Heartland, it's called, as if the chief occupation were love.

"The Americans expect great things of me . . . to show them to the promised land."

And then he went back to Vysoká where the Bohemian Forest edged in closer than the Spillville woods, where people lived knit together, not spread out, not sad to despair. Dvořák lived within the family circle, his wife, his six children. Even his nation was more family than country: a language and a people without an independent government, a culture, not a country. America had best figure out its art forms for itself. Let it study as

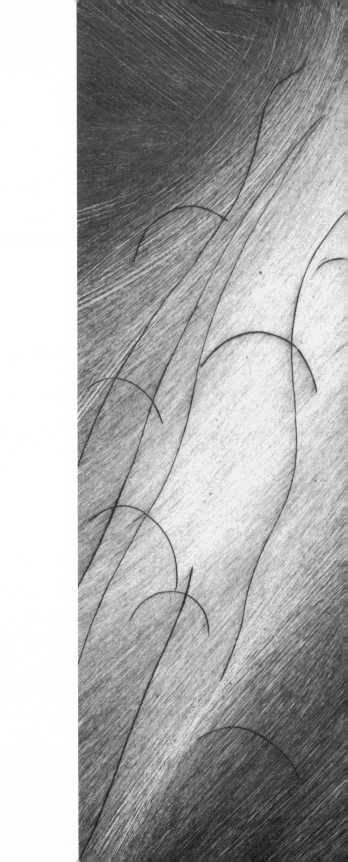

he had: with the birds, flowers, trees, with God, and with its own strange self.

Soon, we will gather for dinner: stiffened catfish, the silver potato, the salad bar where I'll negotiate the French dressing dipper past the plexiglass sneeze shield. Very much at home here, thanks.

And it is beautiful, the gravity of moving water, the stars just starting up in the navy sky. Studying with them. And the silence of these small river towns at night when the traffic on the highway, which crashes like a falls, is well behind us somewhere, people going wherever they must go.

ACKNOWLEDGEMENTS

Spillville is a collaborative meditation, not a work of scholarship. The text relies, however, on the work of various scholars, musicologists and reference librarians, and we would like to acknowledge their efforts.

The direct statements attributed to Dvořák in the text come from his letters or conversations reported by associates or townspeople. These direct quotations are available in a number of sources, including the standard biographies, *Dvořák* by John Clapham, *Anton Dvořák* by Paul Stefan, and *Dvořák* by Alec Robertson, as well as in briefer articles, including the very useful "Dvořák and Spillville, Forty Years After" by Hazel Gertrude Kinscella, published in *Musical America* (March 25, 1933), and the beautifully researched "When Minnehaha Falls Inspired Dvořák" by Lionel B. Davis and Kenneth Carley, published in *Minnesota History* (Fall, 1968).

The quotations from Frank Kapler and most other Spillville residents come from William Malloch's three-part radio documentary "They Remember Dvořák," which was broadcast on Minnesota Public Radio and is in their archive. Anna Kovařík's remarks are from interviews conducted by Lionel B. Davis and Kenneth Carley which are in the Minnesota Historical Society library. We are grateful to them for conducting these interviews.

Pamela Holt of the Hennepin County Library System and Stephen Plumb of the Hill Reference Library were tireless and inventive in their pursuit of books and documents about the Dvořák visit to America.

A number of generous friends gave insightful criticism of the text. They are: Christina Baldwin, Marisha Chamberlain, Carol Conroy, Fran Galt, Margot Kriel Galt, Judith Guest, Phebe Hanson, Rebecca Hill, Edwin Honig, Deborah Keenan, Miriam Levine and Marly Rusoff.

We are grateful as well to Melissa Sorman who suggested Spillville as a subject, and to Clare Sorman and John Roth who were our comrades on the journey there.

EDITOR'S NOTE

Milkweed Editions has a tradition of fostering collaboration. *Spillville* represents an integration of text and image, a mutual exploration by the author and the artist. The collaboration did not end there. The author and the artist, the editors, the printers of the engravings, and the printer of the text spent hundreds of hours planning the limited edition in minute detail.

The type for the text of the limited edition was cast in Bembo by Michael and Winifred Bixler of Skaneateles, New York. The type for the title and the section headings is Felix Titling, specially cast by Norman Fritzberg at the Hansestadt Letterfoundry in St. Paul, Minnesota.

The engravings were printed by master printers Jon Swenson and Bernice Ficek-Swenson, and by Anya Szykitka, at Land Mark Editions in Minneapolis, Minnesota, on a cream-colored Japanese Kitikata paper, and adhered to a heavy gray Rives BFK paper. The colléd pages were sent to Norman Fritzberg at the Hansestadt Letterfoundry to be printed individually on a Vandercook SP-25 proof press and die-cut to the final 12″ x 17″ size.

The forty-one broadsheet-size pages of the limited edition are housed, unbound, in a gold-stamped blue archival presentation box. When the pages are displayed together, the effect is that of a striking, varied landscape of text and engravings.

Patricia Hampl and Steven Sorman continued their collaboration in planning the format for this reader's trade edition.

Patricia Hampl is the author of *A Romantic Education*, a memoir, for which she received a Houghton Mifflin Literary Fellowship, and two books of poetry, *Resort and Other Poems*, and *Woman Before an Aquarium*. Her short fiction, essays and poetry have appeared in *The New Yorker*, *The Best American Short Stories 1977*, *Antaeus*, *The Paris Review*, *MS Magazine*, and *The New York Times Book Review*.

Steven Sorman, an internationally recognized printmaker, has had more than forty one-artist exhibitions of his work, here and abroad. His prints are in many museum, corporate, and individual collections. His bibliography includes Madeleine Deschamps *La Peinture Americaine,* and Richard Field's *Prints: History of an Art: Contemporary Trends.*

818.54
Ha

Northfield Public Library
Northfield, MN 55057